C000258505

Martin Malcolm

Martin Malcolm is a writer, teacher
and storyteller. His other books
for 4Learning include
Isambard Kingdom Brunel,
Animated Tales of the World
and *A Giant in Ancient Egypt*.

Famous People
Sir Francis Drake
c.1540–1596

C3 168820 60   2E

Published by 4Learning
124 Horseferry Road, London SW1P 2TX
Tel: 08701 246 444
www.channel4.com/learning

© 4 Ventures Limited 2003

Written by Martin Malcolm

Education Officer: Anne Fleck
Edited and designed by thingswedo
Illustrator: Jane Tattersfield
Picture Researcher: Jackie Mace
Printer: ESP Colour
Project Manager: Huw Jones

ISBN 1 86215 991 2

Picture credits

The Bridgeman Art Library: page 8
Golden Hinde Exhibition: page 22
© Jason Hawkes/CORBIS: page 4
© Bob Krist/CORBIS: page 18
By courtesy of the National Portrait Gallery, London: cover, pages 6, 16
© National Trust Picture Library: page 17

Gateshead Metropolitan Libraries	
C3 168820 6O 2E	
Askews	22-Sep-2003
J942.05	£5.00

Contents

Growing up

Plymouth harbour today

Francis Drake was born around the year 1540 in Tavistock, Devon. He was the oldest of at least four brothers – and maybe as many as twelve! Francis grew up in violent times. Queen Mary wanted to bring back the old Catholic Church which had been outlawed by her father, King Henry VIII. Mary punished followers of the new Protestant ways, sometimes by burning their leaders at the stake. Francis Drake's father, Edmund, was a Protestant preacher. In 1549 he had to leave Tavistock, perhaps because of his religion.

Stories say Francis and his family ended up living under an old upturned boat near Gillingham in Kent. For some of his childhood, Francis was sent to the seaport of Plymouth to live with a relation, a sailor called John Hawkins. Young Francis began to learn about the ways of the sea and the lands that English people were only just beginning to discover. He longed to sail away himself, to a life of adventure.

'I'd love to sail around the world one day, John.'

Setting sail

Elizabeth became Queen of England when Drake was 18 years old.

In 1558, Queen Elizabeth came to the throne. She favoured the Protestants and life was easier for Edmund Drake, Francis' father. He settled in the town of Upchurch in Kent, where he became the vicar.

Francis soon found work on the nearby River Medway, perhaps as a cabin boy. He learned to use a lead weight on a rope to find out if the water was deep enough for ships to pass safely. He may have learned to use a cross staff to take a reading of the Sun's position, or the compass which showed north, south, east and west. There was also the log line, which told the captain how fast the ship was sailing.

Perhaps Francis saw maps and charts of the world that showed a 'burning zone'. No man could sail past this zone, the old sailors said, because the sea was so hot it boiled and ships caught fire. Francis worked hard and was a keen sailor. When the master of his ship died, so the story goes, he left it to young Francis. With a ship of his own, Francis was ready to seek his fortune.

'Count how many knots are unrolled from this rope in one minute when I throw this log over the side.'

7

A pirate's life

In 1567, Francis sailed with John Hawkins in a fleet of six ships carrying four hundred men. Life aboard ship was hard and cruel and so was the way Hawkins made his money – from selling slaves. He landed on the coast of Guinea in Africa and hunted down local people. They were chained up and dragged back to the ships. Then Hawkins sailed to the West Indies, where Spanish settlers bought slave workers.

King Philip of Spain ruled many places around the world. His power was great and his ships brought back gold, silver and spices from the lands he controlled. King Philip wanted to end Queen Elizabeth's rule and turn England back into a Catholic country. He certainly did not like Englishmen trading in 'his' West Indies.

At Veracruz, the fleet was attacked by Spanish warships. Only the ships led by Drake and Hawkins survived. Francis Drake escaped to England with his ship, the *Judith*. Hawkins got away, too, but later accused Drake of deserting him in the battle. Francis Drake was very angry and swore revenge on Spain.

King Philip of Spain was a rich and powerful man.

In 1572, Francis returned to the Caribbean.
He attacked towns held by Spain and
captured treasure from many Spanish ships.
Francis quickly became feared by the
Spanish settlers. They gave him the nickname
'El Draque' (the Dragon). When Francis
returned to England in 1573 with his treasure,
Queen Elizabeth was very interested indeed.

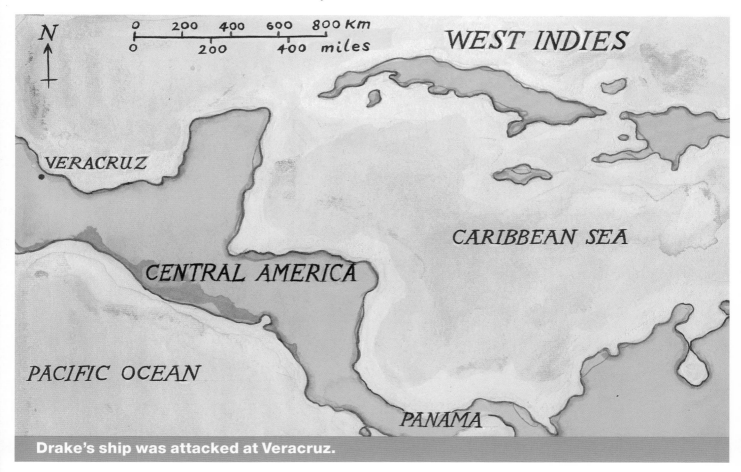

Drake's ship was attacked at Veracruz.

Around the world

'Lo! This is the end of all traitors.'

The Queen sent Francis on another voyage to the West Indies in 1577. Were Drake and his men in search of new lands? Or did they plan to rob Spanish ships of their treasure? Even the men sailing with Drake did not know.

When Francis attacked Spanish ships and stole their treasure, one of his men disagreed with him – and paid the price. Francis had the man, Thomas Doughty, executed. Drake was a very hard man and his crew were often frightened of him.

In those days, people believed Antarctica was joined to South America. They thought the only way from the Atlantic Ocean to the Pacific Ocean was through a narrow and dangerous gap called the Strait of Magellan. Drake led his three ships safely through the strait. But then a huge storm wrecked the *Marigold*, and the *Elizabeth* turned back. That just left Francis Drake's *Golden Hind*.

The *Golden Hind* was blown far off course by the gale. It travelled further south than any European ship had ever been. Drake found an area of open sea between South America and Antarctica. This is labelled the Drake Passage on our maps today.

Drake went on to explore the west coast of North America, claiming it for Queen Elizabeth. He traded with the people living there and at last set out for home. The *Golden Hind* reached England in 1580. After the Queen had taken her share of treasure Drake was still a rich man – and he was the first English captain ever to sail around the world.

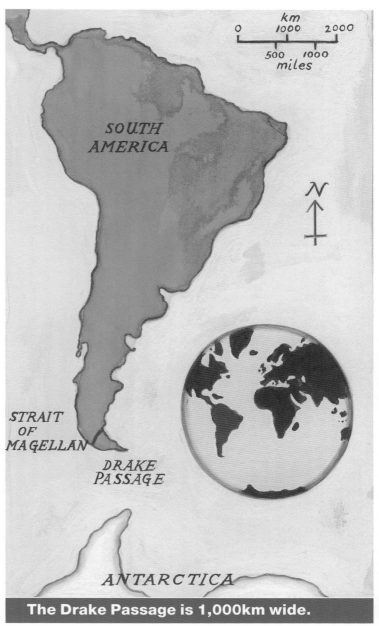

The Drake Passage is 1,000km wide.

The Golden Hind

The *Golden Hind* was moored in London at a place called Deptford. Tourists visited the famous ship.

On 4 April 1581, Queen Elizabeth visited the *Golden Hind*. Francis Drake knelt down on the deck and was made a knight.

'Arise, Sir Francis.'

Armada!

King Philip of Spain began to build up a great fighting fleet, or Armada. The plan was to sail along the English Channel, join up with the King's army in what is now Holland and Belgium and invade England.

To try to stop them, Francis Drake made a surprise attack on the Spanish port of Cadiz. He destroyed around 25 Spanish ships inside their own harbour. He also burned loads of barrels for holding fresh water – without enough water to drink, the ships' crew would be in great trouble. Drake cruised off the coast of Spain, stopping the rest of the Spanish fleet from joining together. Eventually though, his love of gold got the better of him and he sailed away, looking for treasure ships to raid.

Drake's raids gave the English time to get ready. But in 1588, the Armada was sighted off the English coast. Keeping their distance, the English followed the Armada along the Channel. There were several battles, but the English could not break up the Armada's strong defensive shape. They had to stop the Armada from joining forces with King Philip's army.

The Armada ships formed a crescent to protect themselves.

The English used fire to break up the Armada.

When the Armada was anchored off Calais, the English set some of their own ships on fire and let them drift on the tide towards the Spanish. Many of the Armada ships cut their anchor cables to get away. Without anchors, some ships drifted onto rocks and were wrecked. The Spanish defensive shape was broken and the English moved in for the kill. King Philip's plan had failed.

Life ashore and the last voyage

Sir Francis Drake died when he was about 56 years old.

In 1581, Sir Francis Drake bought a great house, Buckland Abbey, near Plymouth. He became Mayor of Plymouth and helped to improve the town's water supply. He also served as a Member of Parliament.

Francis never had any children. He married his first wife, Mary Newman, in 1569 but she died in 1583. Two years later, he married Elizabeth Sydenham. She was said to have been a young, beautiful woman. Francis, the boy who had nothing, had grown to be a very rich and important man. But he was never satisfied. The sea always seemed to be calling him.

Francis made more voyages – but he seemed to have lost his magic touch. In 1589, he tried to place a rival to King Philip of Spain on the throne of Portugal. Drake landed an invasion force and was supposed to support the soldiers with his own ships – but he failed to turn up on time and the battle was lost. Many men were killed. Queen Elizabeth blamed Drake for the failure.

Drake sailed again to the West Indies, dreaming of all the Spanish gold he would capture. But the Spanish were prepared for his arrival and he could not repeat the wild successes of his early life. He fell ill with dysentery. He died on 28 January 1596, struggling from his bunk to put on his armour. He was buried at sea, not far from the places where he had first made his name.

Buckland Abbey

The legend lives on

Stories were made up about Francis Drake's adventurous life. For example, when the Armada was sighted off the English coast, Drake was playing bowls on Plymouth Hoe. He coolly finished his game before setting sail to finish off the Armada.

In many stories, he was given magical powers. For example, it was said that Francis Drake went away on a long voyage. Seven years had passed and his wife grew tired of waiting. She decided to marry again. But Drake heard her from the other side of the world and fired off his cannon. The cannon ball landed in Stogumber Church in Somerset and the wedding was cancelled.

The legend of Drake's drum is also well known. Before his death, Drake is supposed to have promised to come to England's rescue in the future if his drum was beaten. British sailors are said to have heard the drum when the German Navy surrendered in 1918 at the end of the First World War.

A statue of Sir Francis Drake overlooks Plymouth Hoe.

Buckland Abbey is now a museum of Drake's life. A drum, supposed to be his, can still be seen today.

In his own time, Francis Drake was seen as a hero and explorer. Today, some people say he was just a slave trader and pirate, out for what he could get. What do you think?

Legend has it that Drake wanted to finish his game of bowls before defeating the Armada.

A timeline of Sir Francis Drake's life

c. 1540 Francis Drake was born

1540s and 1550s Francis lived with his relation, John Hawkins

1567–1568 Francis sailed to the West Indies with John Hawkins

1569 Francis married Mary Newman

Events in Sir Francis Drake's life

Events in the world

1572 St Bartholomew's Day Massacre of 20,000 Protestants in Paris

1558 Elizabeth became Queen of England

1553–1558 Queen Mary reigned

1545–1548 Spanish discovered silver in Mexico

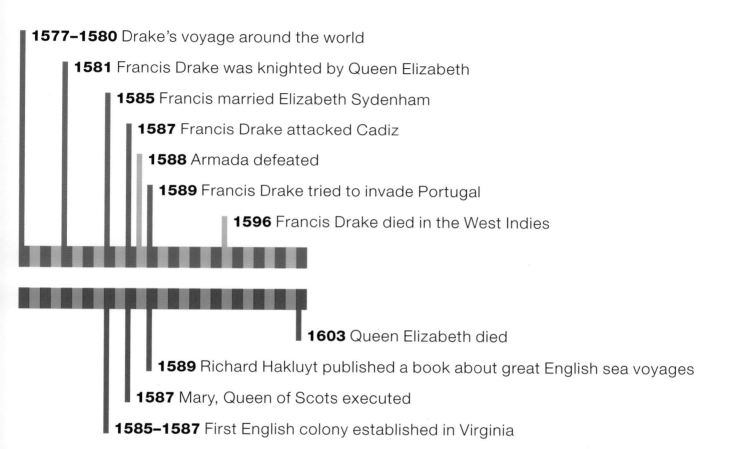

1577–1580 Drake's voyage around the world

1581 Francis Drake was knighted by Queen Elizabeth

1585 Francis married Elizabeth Sydenham

1587 Francis Drake attacked Cadiz

1588 Armada defeated

1589 Francis Drake tried to invade Portugal

1596 Francis Drake died in the West Indies

1603 Queen Elizabeth died

1589 Richard Hakluyt published a book about great English sea voyages

1587 Mary, Queen of Scots executed

1585–1587 First English colony established in Virginia

How to find out more

Books to read

How We Used to Live: Tudor Times; The Spanish Armada; and *Captain Drake's Sea Chest* (Channel Four Television Corporation)

My Uncle Was Sir Francis Drake by Rob Childs (Hodder Wayland, 2000)

Sir Francis Drake by Neil Champion (Heinemann Library, 2002)

Sir Francis Drake and the Golden Hinde by Alex A Cumming (Jarrold Publishing, 1987)

Tudor Explorers (History of Britain) by Brian Williams (Heinemann Library, 1995)

Websites

Golden Hind exhibit
www.goldenhinde.co.uk

Places to visit

Buckland Abbey, Plymouth, Devon

The Golden Hind, St Mary Overie Dock, London Bridge, London

Maritime Heritage Centre, Bristol

National Maritime Museum, Greenwich, London

This is a copy of Drake's ship, the *Golden Hind*

Glossary

anchor *(15)* A heavy iron weight which drags along the sea bed and keeps a ship in the same place.

Armada *(14)* A large fleet of battleships.

Catholic *(4)* A member of the Christian church led by the Pope in Rome.

cross staff *(6)* An instrument used by sailors to measure the Sun's position in the sky.

dysentery *(17)* An infection of the stomach.

fleet *(8)* A group of ships.

harbour *(14)* A safe place for ships to anchor.

Mayor *(16)* The person in charge of an important city.

Member of Parliament *(16)* A person who has been chosen by local people to represent them in parliament.

parliament *(16)* A group of people chosen to represent a country.

pirate *(19)* A robber of ships.

preacher *(4)* A person who teaches and spreads messages about religion.

Protestant *(4)* A Christian who rejects the authority of the Church of Rome.

stake *(4)* A vertical post that has been driven into the ground.

strait *(10)* A passage of open sea between two big land masses.

Veracruz *(8)* A state in eastern Mexico.

voyage *(10)* A long journey made by ship.

West Indies *(8)* A chain of islands located in the Caribbean Sea.

Index

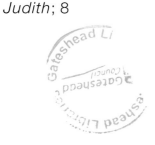
Gateshead Libraries Council